THE BEGINNINGS OF TREES

GERALDINE PAINE

Belfast
LAPWING

First Published by Lapwing Publications
c/o 1, Ballysillan Drive
Belfast BT14 8HQ
lapwing.poetry@ntlworld.com
http://www.lapwingpoetry.com

Since before 1632
the Greig sept of the MacGregor Clan
has been printing and binding books

Lapwing Publications are printed and
hand-bound in Belfast at the Winepress.
Set in Aldine 721 BT

ISBN 978-1-909252-48-6

ACKNOWLEDGEMENTS

My thanks to the editors and judges of the following magazines, anthologies and competitions for publishing, short-listing or placing some of these poems, or versions of these poems:

Agenda, Envoi, Smith's Knoll, Sentinel, The French Literary Review, Equinox, London Grip.
The Basil Bunting Poetry Award, 2010, Second Light Poetry Competition 2010, Buzzwords Poetry Competition 2011, Sentinel Poetry Competition 2012, Canterbury Poet of the Year 2012.
Shape Sifting, Cinnamon Press 2007,
Sixty Poems for Haiti, Cane Arrow Press 2010,
Not Only the Dark, Word Aid 2011.

My thanks go to many colleagues and friends most especially Sheenagh Pugh for her continuing support and encouragement, Sean O'Brien, Susan Wicks, Carole Satyamurti, and Sue Rose for the guidance, help and advice each has given me, the Clink Street Writers Group for their wise words.
And always to my husband, Walter.

Previously Published

The Go-Away-Bird,
Lapwing Publications, 2008.

CONTENTS

For Wal with Love

RELEASE

This must be achieved noiselessly, don't draw
attention to yourself, they will count scores
to keep you longer in the dark. Now, pull
hard. But take good care. The shutters are full
of splinters. Gently. That's it. You can see
green ivy climbing the trunk of a tree,
such fine leaves, so determined; and the slow
water, that's a kind of green too. As though
someone has added milk. The sun is just
reaching the front steps; as it mounts, it must
penetrate this stone grey room. 'Come,' you'll say,
'it's been so cold without you. Every day
I've worked a little more to let you in,
to feel a remembered touch on my skin.'

BUDAPEST 1931
i.m Imre Kinszki 1901-1945

Notice how a low sun
honeycombs the cobbles
with the shadows of ash trees,
how the fence bares broken teeth,
how the boy and girl are held like a breath.

THE ONLY PILGRIMS

We clung in the rubble of bomb-sites,
rose bay willow herb swayed at our feet,

and pigeons, disturbed, resettled to join us
that day, the only pilgrims.

You led me down pockmarked streets
just to see St. Paul's, nothing else.

And I remember a delta of darns
spreading into my ridiculous shoes,

St. Paul's, the great rock among ruins,
your double-lashed, serious eyes.

There are steeples of glass rising now.

RIBBONS

I step inside a house full of square rooms
of beige, they're hard-edged, empty,

the corridors high but light.
I reach one room, very small, its walls

covered with black felt. I look down
at myself. I am transparent,

full of drawers. I open the drawers,
they're a tumble of ribbons

narrow embroidered ribbons,
white with bright colours

like the illumination of manuscripts.
I pin them on the black walls at angles

all over and it's intricate and beautiful
and I made it, the room, from myself.

PILLOW LACE

It started with fishbones picked clean,
clever fingers, a pricked out idea. It started poor

at the feet of mountains. In the Villa Tiguillo
it lies between tissue in drawer upon drawer –

the diamond and daisy, the leaf,
the windmill, the crown head-side plaits,

gimp threads, picots and tallies; at peace
from the spangled bobbins' rattle and clatter,

safe from the perfumed, careless nights
where a dropped glove or the slow fold

of a fan might lead to a hasty unravelling –
a christening robe, the cobweb unrolled

from a lace-maker's pillow; to mayflowers
spilling down wide marble stairs.

THE RED SWEATER

holds me loosely, flows from me
to her, wraps her round me;
blood

lay in skeins
as she sat knitting, saying
red's her colour,

not saying it's mine,
daughter, interloper,
reminder of her past

for the man she ran to,
the one she stayed with,
who watched my sweaters grow.

HER FIRST

It doesn't matter
that the pot plant's spilled,
that the kitten's attacked the dry earth,
rucked rugs into enemies, torn paper limb from limb

or that I wear my dressing gown till noon,
swish in and out of rooms, feel you warm
when we touch on the stairs. They've gone.
Closing in on me, they'd filled every space.

But they had a child.
A gradual smile would creep across her face,
her hand reached out for me once or twice,
and for a blueberry, her first, she'd whisper *psss*
for *please,* echo *yummy* as juice trickled.
Was beginning to know me when they left.

SMOKE

Four panes of clear glass,
an early Victorian sash, separate us;
thick, whitewashed walls keep me
from breathing the Highland air,
as smoke sits in the blue chair.

On the sill
a pile of papers
a folded, striped curtain
and a vase that catches the light
but is empty. Not even thistles,
growing wild in the high grass,
have filled its womanly shape.

.

This is a temporary scene,
a place of absence.

MONIACK MHOR

Today, heather spreads over the moors
like a bruise. There's no pause

in the agitation of grass, in the gale
that sweeps in from the west, bringing tales

of towers collapsing. The Highlands know
about loss since whiteouts of snow

iced five miles into the earth, carving
lochs, since the starving

of crofters when the potato crops failed
and sons, daughters, husbands, sailed

to a world that promised peace;
each life rented. A short lease.

DECHOUKAJ

For twenty seconds
land rippled like water,
cane straw rained down, burning,
and a concrete city fell.

The dust clouds rose
to cover the people, ghost
figures who filled the streets
with their searching.

And stars spilled from the sky.
Women caught them, held them
swaying; congregations
of fitful light.

I hear their prayers,
but trees pulled up by the roots
will never grow again.

Dechoukaj – Haitian Creole for a violent uprooting

QUIELLE
For a young father

In a chapel tidied of history, holiness
peeled from walls, replaced now

by panels of a certain perfection,
a leftover angel watches

as we huddle together
on this site of sorrows,

trying to make sense
of our words.

ROSES OF PICARDY

We speed past fields
as rows of poplars disappear across a land
at peace; no men running, falling helpless
in the mud, no crater scars, no screams.
But the earth has a memory

and a voice. I see my father
sunk in a green armchair singing
to himself the words he knew by heart,
his Irish tenor meant for pals
who never grow old.

LAST LEAVE

> *I've written a Requiem*
> *for an uncle I scarcely knew...*

I'm on my giant's shoulders and he's waltzing me,
whirling me round and round, dislodging

the holly, tearing the paper chains; a toy rabbit
drops onto the cake, *Sweetheart!*

We're all singing, *Heaven... I'm in heaven.*
Below, his friends have wings.

A lopsided grin, fixed in the album now,
froze in January, 'forty-three,'

his Lancaster spiralling down, down
into the ice of a Lincolnshire field.

THE POLOCROSSE MATCH

His tee-shirt billowing, the boy
and his mare career past as one,

the barest touch enough for the charge
of thudding hooves and streaked flanks,

each horse plasticine-easy,
each turn a dressage at speed.

Moments of glory are there.
Hear them in the shouts, the clatter

of sticks crossed in play, see them
as the ball is dislodged, dropped

to earth, scooped up in a net
with a twist of the wrist,

flicked away by the boy;
all the freshness of grass on the air.

COUNTRY GIRL

He rides behind the coach and black-plumed four,
their sons and daughter ramrods by his side;
those horses' hooves he'd shod at six am,
farrier, husband, carrying on, astride
the mare she'd named Storm and tried to tame
by galloping through green cathedral lanes
that smelled of rain and badger setts and earth
disturbed by play. We stand, old friends and some
who simply knew her joy on days like these
when winter's dark undid the strings of light.
Behind the sunlit glass, a family wreath
of trailing leaves becomes a forest floor
that hides her, still and shining girl, from sight.
We cry, she was too young. But so is he.

A FARMER'S EYE

Such a plain, no-nonsense watch:
black strap, Casio digital face,
easily replaceable.

Don't buy me anything fancy.

For those dark mornings
when cattle raise their heads
to hear you, mud-slowed,
treading the ploughed fields.

Simple now, nothing fancy.

But fancy is when you're never late,
always there to offer your hand
as I step down from the train.

COLLARED DOVES

They came to green gardens
from lotus flowers and prayer trees
half a century ago

drawn by an outbreak
of peace and the chance
of cool weather.

They are still here
in the sycamore,
patient as hope

while small birds flap
and squabble below them.
Their calm spreads branches

through the thin sunlight
towards me. It is coloured
dove-grey.

THE LAND

Under the new lawn - chalk,
a hard soil for a tree to survive

the first planting, to grow to be a tree
with branches that filter the sun

and a trunk to tempt a child's arms.
Apples litter the ground, musty, crushed

as we walk through the old orchard
that bends north towards the sea.

A clear run for the winds, here on the ridge,
they've taken the leaves already.

Next spring they'll lift the blossom, comb
the fields of barley, excite horses, lambs.

Today we buy a farmyard, land
where we'll plant the beginnings of trees.

WRITTEN INSTRUCTION 1950

Don't forget to walk on the footpath
if there is one

Look for one hidden by scrub, the one
you need to feel with your bare feet,

the one connecting you to the earth,
the rock, the pebbles, the slub-soft sand,

where the morning sun's been before you;
catch the moment before it cools, grows

clammy, before it's hard to move on;
avoid the cliff edge, it slopes

to nowhere though the view as always
is spectacular.

HORSE SANDS

As we nose into westerlies,
the skies grow overcast

the tide a trickle.
Mud-flats become our beach

where ghost sounds prickle
and microscopic mouths open,

closing as salt slips between shells
to make the Horse Sands sing.

Out on the horizon, near
twin forts with now forgotten point,

white sheets are gathering,
wide-angled, gossipy hulls

battle beyond our reach.
A seal watches, idling.

HONEYMOON

Outside, Atlantic breakers,
inside, a hush of antiques,

the scent of potpourri
from distressed Tuscan urns.

He's sunk in Louis Quinze
the colour of toffee.

We try talking golf,
his Irish roots, vodka martinis.

Leo, it's time for your nap!
Skin-tight in couture,

her eyes sweep us into the grate –
she's priced us. The next day

you buy a tweed jacket, soft
as butter. I polish my shoes.

ONE LAST TIME
Zimbabwe 2008

On the lawn she says goodbye to her Cannas,
the lilies stand tall breathing fire.

I grew them from seed, my John thought them fine.
He'd built her this house, Home Counties-style,

painted it pink, painted her pictures of trees,
the great trees of Rhodesia,

the blue-est delphiniums; a honeymoon view
of the veldt and the kopje they'd climbed.

When she laughs sixty years disappear.
She leads us through rooms

where every curtain is drawn, silver cups
glisten on rosewood and ghosts jostle to speak.

I'll miss all my flowers, she says, *you see
there have always been flowers.*

PASSPORT

She telephones the High Commission here today,
pangas are cutting through the wire as she waits.
Somewhere a farmer lies dying in Zimbabwe,

his blood is spilled for home, love of the veldt, the vlei
of yellow grasses, land he planned to cultivate.
She telephones the High Commission here today

(Her father knew a giant of a man - marked prey,
who'd held them off three hours, to forestall his fate.)
Somewhere a farmer lies dying in Zimbabwe.

She's met with obdurate rules she must first obey,
your prints to be taken in Harare, they state.
She telephones the High Commission here today

to claim her birthright - citizen, not émigré,
the third of five generations she celebrates.
Somewhere a farmer lies dying in Zimbabwe;

(outnumbered a hundred fold, his face grown grey,
he'd leopard-crawled, they'd followed to eliminate.)
She telephones the High Commission here today.
Somewhere a farmer lies dying in Zimbabwe.

DOMBASHAWA
the sacred mountain

Red ochre on pale stone clammy
to touch, the figures dance before us
limbs akimbo, the ancient stories sing.

Below, a boy is waiting drinks in hand;
in the foothills cattle clamber perpendicularly
only a stick to guide them, to move them on,
they are line drawings, rib-thin. Leopards lurk.

Would you know their pulses race – the one boy
with a stick lightly tapping, the other listening
for voices, his skin clammy?

COMPANY

She believed the air was alive with spirits.
She was never alone. She felt them there

keeping her company among the old furniture,
against the peacock walls, in the firelight.

They were warm, not like people say
the dead are. He said she was weird

and mock-shivered.
Sometimes she senses him now.

RESTORATION

The chair is in place, reinstated,
its high Windsor back quite out of proportion

to the rest of the room and yet right.
As though you are restored as you were

before you began to speak in whispers.
When we shared a life of Englishness,

of polished oak, of gold-leafed London squares,
of an Oxford quad bathed in slanting light

where the high, damp grass played host to dreams
and Malvolio crossed a lake illumined by lanterns.

When chairs were chairs.

QUICKSTEP

You said, *we did our best,*
it was the times. Of course it was.
And you were beautiful.

There were blackouts, craters,
the nightly blitz to drive through.
And he could dance, you said.

There was the quickstep, foxtrot, Hutch;
another world and you were young.
Of course you were.

There were the rented rooms, the moonlight
flit, your fleet-footed man and you.
And then there were three.

Where was it you wanted to go?
The end of the line, you said,
a house, a cherry tree.

He wanted the centre of things,
you said. Of course he did.

MISSING

He's in a hotel in the sticks, I can't reach him:
no phone number, not in, he's ill, that sort
of thing; no family's there to console him
and I'm frightened he'll die an outsider, alone.
I wake up, search for a memory. Me, three,

swinging my legs from a high kitchen perch,
licking a spoon: golden syrup, I'm sure;
outside silver boats roll, moored in the sky.
My dungareed, tin-hatted Ma's flying the flag
from her bike. And my twinkle-toed Pa?

The mind's blank, so think.... It's a Sunday.
I'm winding a towel around his wet head,
I've just washed his hair for the third
or fourth time, soon he'll let me do it again.
Can't go now! You stay here with me!

AT THE END
Pinkasova Synagoga, Prague

It's not possible to prepare for this:
birth dates, death dates, surnames in red,

forenames in black, each written so neatly,
alphabetically, divided by asterisks

like stars. Line after line cover the walls.
At the end: Terezin, Treblinka, Oswiecim...

while all around us a cantor sings *kaddish*.
And people clutch stones.

I don't belong here.
But a guide catches my eye, a child then

like me, he reaches out, draws me in,
almost eighty thousand, he says

as his hand sweeps the room.
Two names will be missing, you say

and mention your aunt, cousin,
the train that never arrived.

MILDRED

The drawing room smells rank:
unopened windows, the heat of a fire

left on day and night, velour curtains
drawn against the light. Cats.

They've reproduced without check
in corners, on sofas, upstairs

on beds; the miscarried, aborted,
left among furniture, hidden

in clutter like the old woman
who's forgotten it all

except the piano. A black Steinway
gapes at the back of the chair

where she sleeps, lulled
by her own *Liebestraum.*

He stopped me playing,
was all she said.

THE OLD MASTER LIES
After W.H. Auden

The sculptor carved her, sorrowing and still,
her face upturned, her body gently bowed,
the Holy Mother.

But she would reach out to touch Him,
to feel His skin before all warmth is lost,
to smell the sweetness of Him.

She would embrace His torn limbs
for Him to sense the softness of her cheek
to know her love before the last cry.

The old master lies.

SERENADE FOR KIZHI
After Franz Schubert 1827

We walk in the quietest blue, in green,
a stream threading through the trees,

few birds sing.
Music is in the leaves, in the wind,

calling above the church-without-a-nail,
in our footsteps, a single bell.

On the threshold we stand
in awe of gold, the whispering candles,

old women's sombre stares,
before prayer leads us away

into the green, the blue again,
to breathe in scents of pine,

to watch geese rise, the sun's rays
setting the aspen church ablaze.

TAKING A PHOTO IN VENICE

There's a restless dazzle
as lights unpick the night

and water receives them,
translates them – silver

slinks beside us, shimmies;
we touch silence.

Only the plash of oar reveals
our presence as we glide

a curled serpent through shadows
past secrets of stone

the slight chill of excess;
one flash and the Rialto explodes.

THE COURTESAN

Feed me
one quarter of a *marron glacé*
just one quarter if you will,
I need to savour the soft mouthful,
lick the sugared residue from my lips,
taste the first burst of juice before
I shall know the salt of you.

Do not hurry.
I believe in slowness. Others
may offer you *capezzoli di Venere,*
pane del doge but only I
offer the true *lingue di gatto*
to bring you thirsting
for my cat's tongue.

THE SARDANA

They hand round the *Cap Bon,*
the thin stream pours from bottle

to mouth, the rim never touching their lips.
Then a workman grins at her.

As she tilts back her head to catch
the rough red, he looks away, suddenly shy.

Hens squawk on the rack, feathers drift down,
their owner snores while the carriage grows

smaller, louder, with the wine, the shared cigarettes,
her duty-frees. The Pyrenees turn a parched yellow.

There, where the blast from an ivory horn
once made birds drop from the skies,

she imagines spiralling bodies, a raining
of wings. Sees only the blue.

As she steps from the train into heat
like a locked door, the smell of wet concrete

sharp on the air, bold eyes appraise her,
¡*Hola, Senorita!* ¿*Por qué tan triste?*

She sits at a table alone, tasting fresh words:
Calamari ...Mantequilla ...Alioli...

feels them curl on her tongue.
On the square the circles begin to form.

THE MIDI

An aire
is where you say,
listen to the larks
and I do

Rushing water beneath the window
orchestrates our dreams while children

sleep like dormitories of starlings
and a Virginia creeper sings with bees.

The clock repeats the hour
for a reason no-one now remembers,

from a church tower no-one any longer
sees; owls hunt from chateau walls.

When the self-appointed guard dog
barks, the bullfrog's love call ends;

footsteps brush the street below.
Old men gather. The day begins.

MORNING MEN

They sit on park benches,
hands clasped between knees,

staring ahead, or down at their feet
where smashed glass, fag ends, spilled

Chinese, feathers – the remains of a kill
in the dark or a just-quick-enough flight,

lie quiet among leaves, the night's
noises over. The sun's warm for October.

One West Highland White chases another,
running flat out, in the moment, forever.

These men are on hold, some never
sure what a walk home will bring –

dust gathering on shelves, a ring
left on a dresser, stained mugs in the sink,

the TV still blinking.

HER RILEY

The garage floor's sodden, newspapers
carpet a foreshore of mounds – he scrapes

mysterious labels off cans; Kilner jars ooze
with a brown mess that leaks into his shoes.

It's soft archaeology. *Get some air!*
I plead, imagining circling spores.

But he's just found the Riley, under rugs,
the remains of a fur, magazines, silver cups

almost black and what look like 'Thirties
dance cards, illegible now. A rare beauty's

revealed, racing green, last taxed Nineteen-Sixty.
She'd loved the Derbyshire hills, the moors, distance.

ACTIVITY CLASS

… that I love London so. Ta ra.
He won't let go when the music stops,

only the blue anchor tattoo on his arm
shifts a little. His eyes plead, *mine*

not yours! She's pulling hard
but his claw-like hands cling on.

He's lost seventy years,
under the chair where it's sticky,

or behind the chintz curtain
where his mother waits

he'll be late for his tea again
slap, slap with a slipper.

I'll be seeing you… the carer
sways her hips before him.

Don't like it, want to go home!
The others look up, pom-poms slow,

he drops his tambourine.
How I love you, how I love you….

LEONARDO AND THE WALKMAN 1999

Small drawings of drapery folds
of long-fingered idling hands,
of a boy pared to fine bone.

Lovely pass Beckham made...
three-nil...
what a player!

I think Leonardo'd approve
the quicksilver lad on the wing,
might make him his own.

Galleries call for such stillness;
so much I can't breathe.
The warders pass by

seeing only the pitch,
the home crowd cheering.
I ask the score

more to feel the fresh air
of the game on my skin,
than to care.

INCIDENT

The smell of smoke lingers,
three months after the floor-shaking thud
when he hared down the stairs, shouting.

Flames leapt through the basement grill,
splinters of glass gleamed orange.
You forgot your shoes! she screamed.

but he was pulling a man with bloodied legs
clear, as sirens sped towards them;
hoses began to turn the house grey.

She still listens for the child,
for the yell of a girl who slammed doors;
there's only the creak of a fence

against the Ceanothus and a thrush
cracking open a snail's shell.

THE CREEK

My dad asked, *what's this place then?*
crushing white shells under his feet –

the old ferry car park reeked of fish.
Oare, I said. *Awful, you mean,*

he replied, always the joker.
But he saw mackerel skies, seals

and sailing boats; heard the cries
of fastidious waders picking their way

over sludge that swallows rubber boots
and men; we counted swans like pearls

in the barley, the seventeenth set apart,
scanning the Swale to the sea.

Beyond this slip of silver, freighters
enter Barrow Deep for Tilbury

never a place to linger, engines idling.
There are quieter ways to go.

Mrs Flynn wandered off, she lay down
where the mud was soft and closed her eyes.

Her family and her church missed her,
worried about winds over old bones.

Maybe she followed whispered voices,
felt them kinder than her silent room.

Freya listened to a harsher song,
hung about with children, her little tattoo

grew into a whole wingful of birds
before she left to plummet in the dark.

The city's not sixty miles away,
could be hundreds more

if you're early on the marshes
with the crow-pecked sheep

or breathing hops and apples
near a medieval town

where Londoners and gypsies settle
side by side and a joker died.

A FAMILY CASE

Somewhere by the creek it started,
as he thrashed and swore above a seabird's cry.

Somewhere, among the dog roses he flew,
this weary crop-haired boy.

In court, his earrings catch the light.

Somewhere in the tall grasses she broke him,
holding him in her small cupped hands.

Somewhere along the watery path
he grew old.

In court, she is glittering.

Somewhere among the junk, the clapped-out cars,
he found them, his son, his one-time girl,

somewhere very dark. *I never hurt her,
or the kid, he needed me, that's all.*

In court, the magistrates believe him.

SUDDENLY, MOTHS

She's scared of their wings
the way they fizz against the light,
all that beating

and of shadows on cold walls,
white sheets. He drags on a cigarette,
clears his throat, loudly.

The air teeters.
She imagines her landlady below
in her little, hot room

listening for creaks;
sees the towel he's spread.
Don't hurt me, she says.

COMING OF AGE

She was twenty the first time. A back-hander
across the face, stinging. Her thirties were blurred.

At forty she tries a new eye-shadow, yellow
tinged with brown. Her fingers are gentle.

SHE TELLS ME

There are moments when it is enough
to look at a patch of earth to know peace,
when a clear rise of soil towards branches
of utter complication means simplicity.
When a hopping, hungry bird, alarmed
and shrill, is balm to the damaged mind.
When one corner of the world means more
than it all because, growing or still, it was
always like that, nothing else is so clear.

BLACKBIRD

The bird and I keep company today,
him: hopping, rustling, stealing my blackberries
surreptitiously, he thinks, chancing it anyway;

me: seeing him in a chink of sky, his beak sharp
against a sunlit lace of leaves, hearing him
in the snare-drum roll of wings as he jumps

to a higher branch, seeing me. *You're welcome,*
I say. And he picks his way through the trees,
inch by green inch, feasting the whole afternoon.

PRUNING

September, and I worry about sap still rising in the Lilac tree;
the Quince, whose shrivelled apples he's exposed on bare ground;
      the Buddleia – full cream horns turning brown; me.

But he's a country boy, handy with his secateurs, snip, crack, snip.
Down go the givers of shade and light spreads over the earth.
      Felled branches lie sweetened by rosehips.

Japanese Anemone, isn't it? he points to some stick
that's not bloomed for years. I nod, grinning for all I'm worth,
      remembering pink petals before the Vinca grew thick.

I imagine spring, watching him trim my Choisia bush
a froth of late flowering. *It'll grow back, best thing all round.*
      A path is opening towards me, no need to rush.

PICKPOCKET

It was his eyes, the sly glance
sliding like a snake down my face,
my body sensing a hiding place
for his hands.

It was the heat of him,
the whispering skin, the musk
in the folds of him, the flow,
the skill of him,

but he moved on.

ENGLISH BANK HOLIDAY

Donald Duck holds out his arms, Chinese Duck
every inch of him. *Blue or red?* Whoever's heard

of a duck in a red vest? I choose blue, the colour
of summer, except the rain's tipping down

on this small town's fair like God's called Time.
Oi! Tosser! A blonde, thirteen going on thirty,

calls across to her mates. Leader of the posse left
behind – not cool, she parts little boys like crabgrass,

clump heels battling, leather bum sleeker than a seal,
heading for *Wild Thing.* It seats twenty and swings.

Loudspeakers crackle. The *Helter-Skelter*'s packed-up
and they can't give the *Free Bear If You Lose* away.

It's all done by eight, the stall-holders seem glad.
There's even a local petition to ban it.

HOLDING THE COATS

We could hear shouts, the local boys,
their voices strong, male,
they were just there, so near.

Rude words lobbed over the wall
landed hard on our tennis courts, love
wasn't one. But we wanted much more.

Gym-slipped, giggling, schooled by nuns,
we mingled scents in our dreams: *Brylcreem,
Nuit de Paris, Goya's Black Rose,*

we were All Woman! I had a new kind of ache.
Valerie had an idea, *Let's climb the tall tree!*
Eugènie and Gillian agreed.

I saw myself falling
through thick, jutting branches, unable to stop.
I'll stay here, hold the coats, I said.

ON READING A LETTER TO LARKIN

It was the date, *1953*,
that made me think of leather patches,
corned beef hash, pea-soupers swirling free

down muffled streets, the fug of basement rooms
with Bechet, when I'd long to run from hockey matches
to sink myself in existential gloom

and dream of wearing black like Greco;
for Gérard Philipe to love me more than words could say,
and someone to be waiting in the wings to echo

my desires bang on cue. Before I knew he
was in his prime and didn't dare to prove it, days
he'd pine for rosy, bosomy girls, who'd agree

to make his humdrum doings zing and flare;
girls who'd never be there.

ON THE DRINK

We have a fine balance going, the giving
and taking, the smiles in the afternoon,
the scones and the strawberry jam.

The knock comes at five. It's loud,
not shocking but small spaces disappear
and fill with bulging eyes.

Then furniture staggers, walls lean,
splinters of glass strike carelessly,
words are thrown, uncaught

they slip down between tables. No-one
moves, the dark creeps towards us.
He doesn't leave until nine.

A GAME OF PATIENCE
After Meredith Frampton

She will not move yet
to lift her elbows from the chill slate.
Its smoothness is pleasing.

The cards behave well on it,
they appreciate the perfect circle,
their role in the play. The apples just so,

the fragile corn, each chance by design.
She has set the scene, knowing
the end will define her.

On the terrace, alive with bees,
a saxophone plays only for her.
It is nearly time.

At precisely three he will enter
through pale-green double doors
at the end of this high-ceilinged room.

And she listens
as he turns the elaborate handle,
her hand poised to lay down

the second card she knows is an Ace.
It's the third one that concerns her –
if not the Queen

she'll be lost to a world
of mesh screens, separation,
silence.

PORTRAIT
Edward Thomas by Emil Otto Hoppé

Is it a pose, the desolate look, that studio shot
by Emil? *Put your hands together like so, sir,*
now rest your chin... hold it... and... again.

Ah, the cleft chin: so certain, so driven;
you could seem pugnacious, clever, a dreamer
but see how those full lips give you away.

You needed it all, my beauty, my rare breed,
my dutiful boy. A hundred years on,
the camera can't lie.

THERE WAS A MAN

whose life in cool rooms
where distance was just a stroll from the desk
was his own
once the sprinter who'd always breasted the tape arms raised waving
he tried not to look back
but sat slowly unsure of his weight or the chair's stability
staying all night while the page took his sleep and words clawed
at his clothes
begging for whisky
until he spied bugs in the gathering walls
until he drilled holes in the ceilings to find them
until he'd only talk under trees in the God-given air
until there was no more air.

THERE CAN BE NO CALLING
Detail from the altarpiece of Saint-Just-et-Saint-Pasteur

The smell of apples, a blackbird's song
on the evening air, a touch, a smile, my love

there is nothing left but time. This place is blind,
yet our eyes still stare. We are earth-hardened.
No words can reach us; there can be no calling.

Oh, teach me the inevitability of loss.

We have been painted in the colours of sin:
the vine greens, the wine reds no longer savoured.
Will they flake, fall from us once regret is done?

Geraldine Paine

Geraldine Paine